DHARMA IN LIFE'S WAYS AS KARMA .

DHARMA IN LIFE'S WAYS AS KARMA NECESSITATES WAYS FOR STRICT ADHERENCE.

GADHADHARAN PUNATHIL

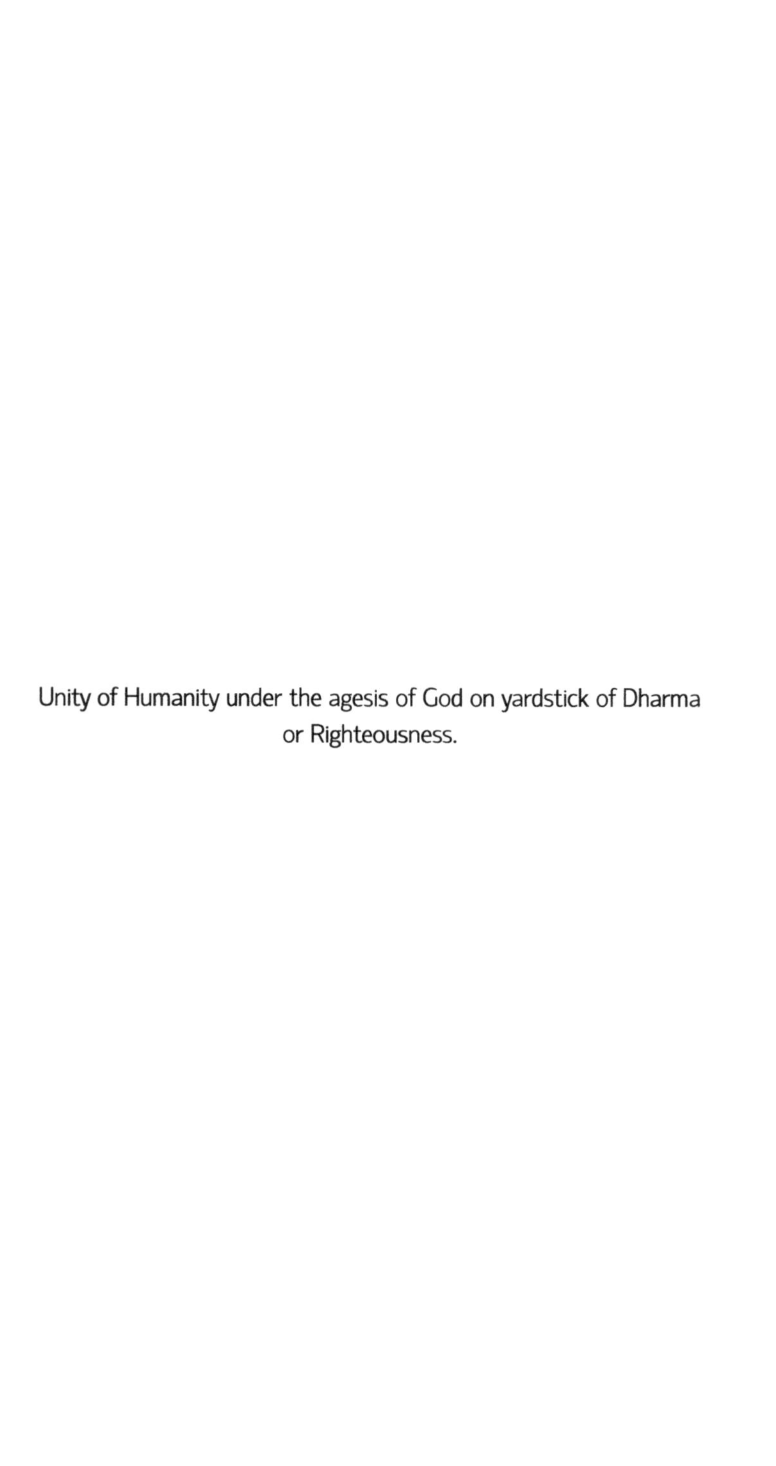

Unity of Humanity under the agesis of God on yardstick of Dharma or Righteousness.

Contents

Foreword

Dharma in life's ways as Karma that is Dharma in everyday activities brings the sequelae of innumerable issues and situations cropping up requiring ways and means for strict adherence to Dharma instead of succumbing and falling, failing in ones dutie's as a human being. Author tries to bring out the ways for these ends that are as perceivable from the rich experiences of humanity's Journey to yonder levels of progress as destined. Hope By God's grace the rich and inspiring experiences of humanity viewed in the context of present situations will enable one to steer clear of all fetters and thrive in the quest for Dharma .

Preface

Dharma in life's ways as karma is an endeavor by The author to bring out the concepts and ways contrived and propounded by humanity in upholding and adopting the concepts of " Dharma in life's ways as Karma " by Divine logic embodied in the Great spiritual manifestations decipherable from the centuries of humanity's progress beginning with the advent of ancient civilizations, especially with an emphasis in Hindutva evolution, adherence and establishment of Dharma in life's ways for Humanity's spiritual as well as material progress enabling anyone to follow the path of Dharma in life's ways with simple changes and adoptions of goals in everyday life.

Gadhadharan Punathil

Acknowledgements

"Eashwara Guruveaa". "God The Teacher ".

Prologue

When 0ne endeavors to adhere to the path of " Dharma in life's ways as Karma ". Innumerable obstacles and difficulties crop up impinging on for stultifying the strict adherence to the Dharma's way of life. How these fetters were overcome by Humanity is there for anyone to perceive. If one peruses the history of humanity's progress to the present day it becomes obvious that These realities are there for anyone to perceive or are perceivable from the Historic realities and spiritual scriptures. This is tried to be brought out by the Author for humanity's good and peaceful progress in happiness. Maybe these will be of use to everyone in day to day lives successes and progress in sustainable happiness.

CHAPTER ONE

Dharma is as perceivable Righteousness or Good, especially as is evident in perusing my earlier book "Dharma in life". This book " Dharma in life's ways as Karma" is in continuation of my earlier scribbling "Dharma in life so as to bring about the necessities required for the full adherence to the concept of Dharma in life. Dharma in life's ways for goals is actually Karma or activities acts and deeds in everyday life's pursuits. In perusing the progress of humanity from The Era of The Rule of Jungle to the Rule of Law and finally, to the yet unachieved Rule of Love it becomes evident that Humanity savagely roamed the globe without any Dharma or Good in them as Evil beasts in their early stages of evolution to the present times Modern human being. In these ancient times, no rules of ethics or law were there to govern the conduct of human beings even with respect to their relationships with one another. Even in genders relationships, it's seen to be rather savage and evil bringing in the concept of darkness and evil befallen. The early man in those days wakes up from sleep and finds a female nearby stalks here grabs her and rapes her then lets her go. She runs away and gives birth to a baby someplace and brings the child up without any connection whatsoever to the father. This cycle goes on and on and finally, Humanity progressed from food hunter to food gatherer and cultivator coming together in clusters or groups bringing into existence clans and society. This is when rules and laws for the good of the group or society become necessary and comes into existence. This is an important stage in the evolution or Journey of humanity from the evil dark days of evil to the Good rule of law or Dharma. Here one finds that rules were brought into being as to secure the safety and security of females. It was during this period that women and their well-being, welfare, and security were given importance. This brought about the concept of wives of Males and children of a male and females bringing into existence the family concept and further laws for the welfare, well-being safety, and the good of the family. This is the point where Males' and females' togetherness and importance for securing the peaceful[progress in happiness for humanity comes up recognizing the reality that men and women are meant to be together as consorts if progress in peace and happiness is to be achieved.

As is evident that The Holy Bible says God created Adam from the soil in his own resemblance and finding Adam lonely put Adam to sleep and created Eve out of a rib of Adam to be his consort and partner in life so as bring in an end to Adam's loneliness. This inference substantiates God's intention to or God's wish that Men should combine with women so as to fulfill life's goals and it's for this natural consortium or to be consorts that genders are created by God bringing in an irrefutable reality that naturally it's only marriage or consortium of Humanity's genders that is permissible. This is a step in streamlining good in life for achieving sure progress to contemplated goals. In this context, one should remember that "It's said that " Man will rise above himself surpass himself and reach up to God". Reaching up to God is salvation or the ultimate progress in the fulfillment of human life for which a human being takes birth. Salvation is not death its immortality or eternal life in peaceful happiness. Holy Bible speaks of God PROMISING eternal life in happiness. The Vedas says, that the progress of humanity is from Asathoma Sadgamaya. ...Thamosama Jyothir Gamaya....Mrithyorma Amrutham Gamaya" Loka samastha sukenova bandhu..Aum Shante Shante Shante Shante hee ...Meaning... That the progress of humanity is From " Evil to Dharma (Good) " Froom, Darkness to Light, and from Death to Immortality through the Amruth or elixir of life" These realities substantiate that Hindutva concepts propagated peaceful happiness immortality to a human being and was in prevalence much before the advent of Jesus Christ and Holy Bible. On an evaluation of these one can conclude that The purpose a human being manifests is for excelling in life and reaching the goal enjoined by God . Thi is the duty of every human being coupled with the duty to preserve .protect and sustain himself and the universe. In these endeavors, one can say that coming into a union of the genders as a family is given much importance.

It is said that family is the building block of society. Societies that of a Nation and Nations constitute the world. As a corollary when families are besmirched, it reflects upon the well-being safety, and security of the society, and consequently, it's the Nations that suffers reflecting on the world at large. The coming of the families and its prominence brings in the importance of preserving well-being. welfare, security, and safety of the families. The first family as can be deciphered and ascertained from the Holy Bible is that of Adam and Eve. God created Adam and then Eve to be partners and spouses in peaceful progress in happiness and immortality. How this first family was besmirched is a lesson everyone should remember so that everyone becomes aware of the tactics used to stultify family by Satan or Satanic forces enabling all to take measures and contrive ways for safeguarding their families. Its a fact that is ascertainable on a perusal of The Holy Bible that Satan, while Eve was alone, approached her and by falsities and lies convinced Eve that God is a lier and that if she ate the forbidden fruit she will get similar powers as God and that God does not like her getting powers akin to God so God has asked not to eat the forbidden fruit. Eve alone was easily won over by Satan and Eve went against God by eating the forbidden fruit. Eve later persuaded Adam also to eat the forbidden fruit thus committing the first sin against God with consequences all humanity is even now suffering. Thus it is evident that ladies are vulnerable when left alone to do the unwanted. It's because of this vulnerability that in Earlier times it was advised that ladies should be chaperoned by someone and should not go alone anywhere. Even now in present times, this is a reality. For Dharma, it is a necessity that Males and females of human genders should go hand in glove together in unison. Surging forth in unison together brings in the necessity of mental attitudes and aspirations going uniformly together necessitating the attributes of similar attitudes and aspirations facilitating the going together in unison. The question is whether it is possible to find two persons having similar qualities in all respects. In God's creations, one cannot find two individuals or things similar in all respects and aspects. Even two grass blades differ in many aspects. How can two or more individuals go on together even though they are having different aspirations, qualities, desires capabilities, capacities, and goals Nowadays we see the coming into being of United Nations Organisations an organization of different differing nations coming together and working for the common goal of common good basic rights and welfare fo all nations even though they have different wants aspirations and necessities. Its the necessity and goal of the common good or Dharma that brings together nations and goes in unison sacrificing many so as to accommodate basic necessities welfare, well-being safety, and security of Humanity and Nations in general. Even in the family, it's bringing about a union of two different persons having different aspirations, desires capabilities, etc on common goals of family life security, peace, and happiness. This is brought about not by two persons standing by their respective sides but by moving over to accommodate each other giving up or sacrificing many personal desires or aspirations so as to bring about a coming together for common goals of family, happiness, etc. This common yardstick can only be something that is acceptable for all. It is in this context that Dharma assumes importance and comes into prominence. It is only Dharma that is the only common factor acceptable to all. No one will desire or work for bringing about bad in oneself or in one's life or ways. It's only Good that all desire, want, and aspire in life. Making the good of all or two the Goal of coming together is the only viable or acceptable parameter for any one or more persons coming together. People coming together for bad purposes will bring in bad to humanity and will be dealt with sternly when apprehended more so as everything that brings in bad is a crime also. This is where Dharma, righteousness, or Good comes in and supplies the necessary yardstick for coming together of individuals, People, and nations.

Humanity has experimented with polygamy, polyandry and is finally in the process of experimenting with one man one women law as family law a; over The world. The law of marriage and family prevalent in India nowadays is imposed by The British and is not strictly Hindutva family laws. Even though India is the birthplace of Hindutva many of its laws are as contrived and enforced by The English British and are continued even now. Now faced with these realite4s one grasps to find out what is the family laws of Hindutva. Muslim laws allow males to marry up to four wives. This can be done only with the permission of all wives with a further condition that all should be treated, sustained, preserved, and protected equally. In the ensuing situations, how does one find out the correct family laws prevalent among Hindus as Hindutva family laws. It is a well-known reality that Hindutva ensured equality for women in all matters and Hindu women are paramountly superior in chastity valor and humanness from ancient times. Even in 1857, it was Rani Lakshmi Bai. Rani of Jhansi the wife of the then King of Jhansi who stood out and fought against the British showing to the world that Hindutva postulated and provides equality to women. The familial bonds were considered sacred. Husband and wife's bond was a sacred bond and both were required to be completely faithful and sincere towards each other. There were earlier instances of the Wife voluntarily committing Sathi or suicide after the death of her husband. This was earlier done out of love and melancholy. But these practices later were enforced with force by the priestly class making it involuntary and bringing in evilness. Sathi was later abolished and made punishable. Sree Krishna the incarnation of God who manifested on Earth for showing a way in reestablishing Dharma seeing DHARMA DEGENERATE AND ADHARMA flourishing is an Avathar with unthinkable powers and Superhuman entity as is seen from the simple fact that Just holding a hand above and raising the little finger brought in The Mighty all destructive weapon of Sudarshana chakra on to Sree Krishnas little finger. Sree Krishna is said to have sixteen thousand and eight wives. Naradha is a sanyasi who is an Angel capable of going anywhere as he pleases. It is said that Naradha has a doubt as to what Sree Krishna is doing with these sixteen thousand and eight wives. To quell his doubt Naradha went to Sree Krishna's first wife to see what Sree Krishna was doing Narada found that Krishna was there doing things with his wife. Then Narada went to second wife and saw Krishna was there also. With every wife Sree Krishna was there doing this and that treating them equally. On seeing this Naradha was overcome with remorse and fell on Sree Krishna's feet begging pardon for doubting The Lord Sree Krishna. This is what a Hindu should do with wives Even though Hindutva does not prescribe the number of wives one should marry. It is always dependent on the capacity to treat wives equally in all respects and aspects. There may be persons who won't be satisfied with one wife and compelling these types of persons to go on with one wife will be doing injustice to his wife as well as himself so if The wife and husband decide that there should be a second wife who can be treated by the couple equally they can opt so and that is how family laws stand. Sree Krishan is Amighty's Avathar who is capable of superman powers and levels of actions. But we Ordinary people will not be able to do these things. We, ordinary persons, can't even be able to cope with one wife In such situations thinking of innumerable wives as Sree Krishna had so is madness and unholy. This is the family law of Hindutva as decipherable from Hindutva life's ways.Anyone who si a little acquainted with Hinduism knows Lord Shiva The lord and Deva or the Angel of destruction and Death. Mahadeva's consort wife is Parvathee a chaste modest noble lady Divine Mother who is personified, revered, and worshipped by all.Parvathy has only one husband and consort and that is Mahadeva or Lord Shiva. But when Parvathee is bothered by Evil Rakshas or Evil persons and entities she in anger gets herself transformed into " Kalee ",the ultimate in destruction of Evil and preservation of Righteous or Good.Once Kalee matha's Thandava of destruction and killing ignites and gets started No one can stop Divine Mother Kalee matha . Only Mahadeva can cool her down. " Aum namoo Kalee mathayea nama". Many profligate and licentious people especially Satanic group ladies fraudulently and deceitfully impersonate and takes up the role of Kalee for espousing deceitfully indiscriminate promiscuous sex destructive of family Love, security, and unity thereby shattering family life. This is the falsification of Hindutva concepts for personal gains and evil . Kalee or Parvathee has only one husband and consort namely Lord Shiva and does not indulge in indiscriminate sex nor is it vouchsafed by Kalee matha . Damn those who besmirch Kalee Matha .

Bad is Evil and harmful to people persons and humanity in general. Telling falsities in order to deceive others to gain an advantage and cause them harm by breaking God's dictates or laws of nations is a bad deed. Deceiving others by falsities and gaining an advantage is not smartness its deceitful fraud and cheating an evil sin unpardonable. Smartness is doing things or assignments easily quickly and correctly. This one comes to deceit and falsities being explicitly sins pushing humanity to evil and perils. Everyone knows that lies, falsities, and deceit are sins forbidden.Falisites and lies are common perils endangering humanity in general and have to be nipped in the bud as harmful for humanity's progress in peace and happiness.The things harmful pushing humanity to perils bringing in the duty to speak out and The all-pervading concept of " Right of all and everyone to intervenance in common problems faced by humanity in general or as a whole cropping up anywhere in the universe ". This is a necessity and compulsory basic duty of every human being to speak out and try to bring to an end or mitigate common problems maligning humanity ensuing of the common good. The realite3s being this, Is there a time or way to JUSTIFY LIE's AS A COMPULSORY DUTY and UPHOLD falsities and deceitful ways in life. Prima Facie the answer has to be, that there is no scope for falsities or lies in Human life except with the repercussions of sinful retributions.The answer to this predicament is available when one peruses the Great Indian spiritual Epical logic embodied in MAHABARATHA'S "GEETOPADESAM". Which is a Flowing of divine logic in the form of advice from Sree Krishna to Arjuna and also from the instances of Sree Krishna's advice in the course of the Great Mahabaratha war. Here what is relevant is the war scenario of Mahabaratha. The Kauravas led by Duryodhana and the mighty warriors are the Mighetest Army that Pandavas or five brothers have to face and defeat so as to get back their prestige and kingdom.In the war, Even Sree Krishna's army is given to Kauravas. Sree Krishna is with Pandavas as the charioteer of Arjuna that too with a vow of prohibition not to take up weapons or fight on one side. It is there that on seeing all relatives, grandfather, and even Guru(Teacher) Dhronacharya lined up to fight Arjuna was taken over by remorse and started lamenting why he should or The Pandavas FIGHT AND kills ALL RELATIVES FOR GETTING THEIR RIGHTS ESTABLISHED AND ARJUNA

LAID DOWN HIS BOW AND ARROW CRYING IN DISSAPOINTMENT. IT WAS AT THIS JUNCTURE IN THE MIDDLE OF THE BATTLEFIELD TWO ARMIES LINED FACING EACH OTHER THAT SREE KRISHNA BY THE DIVINE LOGIC OF GEETHA DISCOUSURES REINVIROGORATES ARJUNA to take up weapons and fight to nip in the bud and eradicate the evil for the common good of humanity.Here4 one finds that Arjuna is in the place of a human and Sree Krishna the reincarnation of God manifesting in the world seeing the degradation of Dharma and rise of adharma .In the war that is fought royal strictly by the principles of Dharma Yudh one finds that Th Evil, Kauravas [aractising deceit and treachery going against the concepts of Dharma yudh of even resuming fight only after a new weapon is given to the opponent if he breaks his weapon and ending all fight at sunset, etc and securing gains and quick advantages in illegal ways and means. Fed up with these adharmic ways and evil deceitful ways of Kauravas. The Pandavas gathered together in a conference presided over by Sree Krishan on evaluating these evil false deceitful ways and means employed by the Kauravas for securing an advantage adharmic ways They sought the advice of Sree Krishna as to what is to be done to face these deceitful ways and means employed. Sree Krishna by Divin logic said that Deceit and lies can be employed without sin only to enable Dharma to triumph when faced with adharmic deceitful activities. For Good or Righteousness to win when faced with deceitful activities for gaining an advantage anyone and everyone are entitled as a matter of right to resort to deceit and lies. This is with the ultimate purpose of establishing public good that once evil or deceitful ways enabling the triumph of Evil succeed it will be ravaging perils for humanity in general. It is on these principles of deceit for deceit enabling Good or Dharma to triumph that Pandavas carried forth the war and won. Arjuna's son Abhimanyu was treacherously stabbed from the back by Jayadhara and killed inside the padmavuha assembling of The Kauruva army. On hearing of the death of his beloved son, Arjuna took up a vow that he will kill Jayadharatha before sunset failing which commit suicide. Jayadharatha went in hiding and could not be found anywhere. It was fast nearing sunset and was nearly evening... Sree Krishna smelling the precarious situation of events held his hand high with little finger pointing upwards and lo came the Sudarshan chakra onto the finger. Sree Krishna using the mighty weapon of Sudarshan chakra covered the sun and brought about a situation as of night. All cried out ho it's was sunset and night, Arjuna has not been able to kill Jayadharatha and has to commit suicide. A bid funeral pyre was lighted and a stage was built for Arjuna to jump into the fire and commit suicide. The fire was burning high and Arjuna ascended the stage with Sree Krishna as if to jump into the funeral pyre. Jayadharadha hearing that his arch-enemy was about to commit suicide by jumping into the fire came out of hiding so that he could rejoice and enjoy seeing in person the death of his arch-enemy. Jayadharadha was standing in the crowd for seeing Arjuna's death ..Sree Krishan saw him and what Sree Krishan did folks, Sree Krishan withdrew the Sudarshana chakra covering the sun and lo sun came out suddenly bringing in broad daylight. Sree Krishan pointed out Jayadhradha to Arjuna and told him to shoot Jayadhradha ..Arjunas arrow swiftly found its target and lo Jayadhradha was dead before sunset. Then in another instance, folks it goes by That The mighty warrior and Guru of all Pandavas and Kauravas Dhronacharya siding with Kauravas and wreaking havoc with enemies armies killing them enmass could be killed only when he laid down his weapons voluntarily. Dhronacharya will lay down his weapons only if and when his con Ashwathamav dies. Whatever Ashwathamav could not be found and killed So folks know what the Pandavas did They named an elephant Ashwathamav and Bheem with a single blow of his mace killed the elephant in front of all.All started saying that Ashwathamav is dead. The news reached Dhronacharya's ears but The mighty Dhroancharya uttered Only if Dharmaputra The eldest of the Pandavas said that Ashwathamav is dead will he lay down his weapons. Dharmaputra kept silent of the word elephant and said that Ashwathamav is killed by Bheema. Dhronacharya on hearing this laid down his weapons and Arjuna swiftly killed him with an arrow at the instance of Sree Krishan.These are instances that come to light when deceit and falsities' ways were effectively and rightly used to see that Good triumphs over evil deceitful persons' ways and means. From these Divine logic, one can safely assume conclude and infer the reality that Deceit and falsities can be used without sin only to see that Dharma triumphs over evil and their deceitful falsities ways.This is a pointer of the conceptual evolution of ways intended in furthering Dharma in life's practical situations and dispositions. This and other ways earlier discussed are ascertainable from the course of the progress of humanity from the era of Jungle to the present times.

What use is there in strictly adhering to the Dharmic path. Is it sheer foolishness . Isn't it better to grab greedily anything and everything that one aspires even if it's others' wives and possessions. It is in these situations God's arrangement of natural forces operates without fail as

"Karma Yoga's" inevitabilities consistently and uniformly bringing in the same repercussions on oneself as one perpetrates surely and certainly as substantiated by Sir Issac Newton's third law A scientific principle always certain to crop up perpetrating its effect on the earth. So folks we have to again go back to the Era of Mahabaratha long before the advent of Jesus Christ, Mohammed The prophet, or other Prophets so as to enable one to unfurl the outcome of adhering to Dharma in life whatever the situations and circumstances. For this one has to follow the life of The eldest of The Pandavas namely Dharmaputra or Udhirishta. It is said that Dharmaputra is the son of Yama or the Angel of death. DharmaPutra always adhered to good ways and means. After winning the war of Mahabaratha the Pandavas reigned for eons as Kings. After Sree Krishna left this world Pandavas decided that it was time that they went on their life's ways or vanaprastha. They entrusted the Kingdom to Parakshit and started their Journey of vanaprastha. After some time the brothers one by one started to fall and die. Panchali and other ladies all died. Finally, only Dharmaputra is left alive and he goes on and on. A dog afflicted with skin disease is the only one accompanying Dharmaputra. They together ate food and went on and on finally it's said that a chariot from heaven come down and stood before Dharmaputra and informed him that he is to abode the chariot and is welcome to heaven in body and soul intact as a human being. DharmaPutra was spellbound and astonished and while about to bode The chariot looked around to see the dog who had given him company all through while alone, standing with him wagging its tail. Suddenly Dharmaputra called the dog and asked to get into the chariot with him but the charioteer interdicted and told Dharmaputra that he has no orders to take the dog and can only take Dharmaputra in the chariot. Dharmaputra stood adamant that he won't board the chariot except with the dog. The charioteer could not go back without Dharmaputra but Dharmaputra won't come except with the dog. There ensued a standoff bringing all All Angles and God into a predicament. Finally, as Dharmaputra wouldn't relent in these testing ordeals of Triumph for Righteousness, it's said that The Dog assumed its original form of Dharmadeva or Yaman The angel of death who could go anywhere including in the chariot. Thereafter Dharmaputra and Yama boarded the chariot and ascended to heaven in salvation of blissful peace and happiness in immortality. These are perceivable from the Hindutva experiences of Humanity bringing in the enlightenment upon one and every prudent reasonable person that Dharma in life strictly adhered to without fail is the only way for salvation or realization of God bringing in the realities of Blissful happiness in immortality. In adherence to Dharma in life bring in situations where doing one thing will bring in a little misery as compared to doing the other will bring in catastrophes. Dharma enjoins one to do that which will bring in less or namesake bearable miseries when confronted with such situations.

In present times one finds nations managed as if they are companies.Vizkids from multinationals comes into control of every aspect of Governance of The Country and they dictate means and ways to see that The country or Countries are managed in a profitable way. The accounts showing a surplus becomes importance or is given prominence and all humanness and service orientation for people are given up in place of profit to Government. Nowadays we find public utility services whereby Government provides basic necessary essential services to people are sold to companies and private hands for furthering The Profit motive of the Government intending to secure a profit-oriented economy instead of vibrant machinery subserving the people for their well being and welfare. Actually if one understands the nature of Public utility services it becomes manifest that They are worth their value more than in Gold even if they make a little loss as they provide essential services to people so as to enable secure their welfare and wellbeing. The mere securing of breakeven in these public utility services is an excellent performance. These profit-motivated attitudes in all aspects of life has radically changed human nature also making human beings less humane and more business-oriented impinging upon the viability of humanness and human love thereby fettering and stultifying the ultimate progress of humanity yet to be achieved. Nowadays to find true human love one has to search much. Everyone is trying to grab some money by hook or crook. One can find this even among laborers. They work for ten days when the same work can actually be finished in five days. In Government offices also one finds these attitudes rampantly employed to drive in an illegal gratification. These types of Government officials finds faults with everything and come up with all errors and faults driving people from pillar to post making them visit the offices, again and again, driving people crazy. All these comes to an end when they get some money as bribes. On getting money all errors and faults vanished and everything is alright and made available easily. The petroleum prices go up and Government is pressured to hike the prices but when the prices comes down commensurate price decrease does not get affected, The hiked price stays as it is fleeching the people of their hard-earned money. In all these cutthroat efforts of even Governmental organizations and wings for-profits what is lacking is Dharma or Good of people. Dharma has vanished and everything are measured in terms of the money they bring in earn or make. The touch of humanness is vanishing fast making people evil denuded of the human love and humanness prone to evil savage ways. Deceit and fraud have become a way of life of many and are even tolerated and encouraged by even some law enforcement agencies. Earlier in the Calicut railway station on the easter side of the overhead pathway, there was a big board on which was written: " When lies have become a way of life revolution is speaking the truth".This is a pointer to how much Good has vanished and social degradation ensued. In times like these, the only way to secure the welfare and wellbeing of people is to manage nations in a Dharmic holistic way so as to make paramount the happiness wellbeing, and welfare of the people giving ago by to profit striking. In these circumstances a breakeven in accounts of Nations is excellent. The happiness of people if achieved in spite of A little deficit is a very good levels of management of nations. Most Economic principles are stultified and concocted to suit the interests of the rich and wealthy so as to enable them to enhance preserve and protect their riches. Think of it nowadays because of the parrot learned stultified principles of economics employed by Hightech Psuedo intelligent Finance ministers giving a go by to happiness wellbeing and welfare of people Majority of Wealth is concentrated in the hands of the few. Nowadays one finds that the Majority of wealth is in the hands or controlled by say about three thousand billionaires in the world. Only Billionaires can secure loans to augment their wealth and enhance it for paltry interest say a four percent interest per annum when they earn thousands of percent as profit using this capital. Think of it this capital comes from the vast general public savings with Government and governmental organizations secured on throwaway interests. Even geriatrics‘ hard-earned savings on which they rely in the evening of their lives for day to day expenses are given paltry interest. Over and above this crooked profit-oriented management of economics the Dharmic concept of " Reasonable returns for peoples hard earned money and efforts " has to be given predominance and adopted in nations' economic management so as to achieve the goals of Ultimate progress of Humanity in peace and Happiness.

The activities acts deeds, and doings of a human being in everyday life are what is Karma in life's ways and form the basis of a human being's ascendence to lofty heights of progress. It is the cumulative effect of a Human being's Karma's or activities that determine the Human being's destiny or faith. The enlightenment that manifests from the Hindutva concept...

Karmaneyea vadhekaraseyea
Maphaleasu kadhachena
Ma Karmaphalea durbuhu
Mathea sankochuava Karmane.

Meaning...... "One's duty is to preserve in doing one's Karma without any doubts never thinking of its fruits or returns "

These verses are from Bhagavat Geetha wherein Sree Krishna advises the desolationed Arjuna unwilling to fight his relatives all arried on the side of Evil, To do his duty of fighting the evil without being concerned about the results or repercussions. These Divine logic as a corollary Brings in the reality that A Human being is endowed with the capabilities and has the power to mold and control his

Karma so as to see to it that his activities, acts deeds and doings are all in consonance and accordance with Dharma thereby making his destiny manifestly ascertainable and determinable by himself. This is how Man has to rise above himself ..Surpass himself and reach upto God. Here Arjuna could having regard to the fact that all his opponents are his own kith and kin and even Grandfather, refuse to do his duty of fighting the evil and thereby stultify Dharma bringing in adverse retardation of progress by nonperformance of duties. This way a human being is endowed with and has the choice of doing one's duty or not doing the same and thereby determining One's destiny. these practices of controlling and channeling one's deeds appear to be reasonably sensible and practical as anyone knows that one's thoughts and desires come and go in mind every minute and controlling thoughts are rather not possible. One can money concentrate on one thought so that others won't come up much even them others will crop up in between. Thi sis the nature of one's or human's mind and is a necessity to arrive at Just and correct decisions. When one goes about solving a particular problem one can experience all sorts of thoughts of possibilities in respect of that problem cropping up so as to enable one's mind to weigh in and reason of the possibilities and come to a correct decision to solve the particular problem. If all sorts of right and wrong thoughts do not come to one's mind then we become incapable of reason away the different thoughts and arriving at a correct one to make it practicable;e and thus succeed, So it's futile to control one's mind. Let the thought good, bad, and whatever comes and go in the mind Never mind but Comrades mind your actions activities, deeds, and acts ...Deeds and your activities of course you can or one can control and channel.

It's the deeds and activities that matter and that are under one's power and capability to control and determine. The bad thoughts and desires should not be converted into acts and activities. Only the good ones should be practicalized and made realities enabling oneself and humanity in general to progress in peace and happiness.

Another aspect of human life enabling one to make practical Dharma is one's strength and grit. A human being is as you are aware is the coming together of the elements and particle of God. Sole need s only Dharma in lives ways as its nourishment and exercises but the human body needs food drink some comforts, maybe some luxuries, exercise as well as sex for wellbeing. One has to nourish sustain and maintain one's body in all ways possible in a righteous way. Merely looking after the soul's needs and renouncing everything else as nonessential and anathema is foolishness. Without a healthy body, one cant go on with the Dharmic ways in life and means strictly in such ways so as to overcome obstacles with grit and strength. Only with strength will grit manifest. So eat anything edible and good for one's body. Sustain, preserve and Maintain health with proper exercise so that grit naturally come in when necessary to uphold Dharma in all always possible. The Somanatha temple in Gujrat is famous for its riches and sanctity. Even in ancient times Thousands of people and hefty priests thronged the temple premises always. Mohammedans Kings from the Afghanistan side used to invade India, especially Gujrat so as to plunder and steal the wealth of Temples and Somanatha Temple was a constant attraction for these dacoits' life Mohamedans. Mohammed of Ghor and Mohammed of Gazhni were the prime invaders who plundered the Somanatha Temple and robbed the riches. They came in houses say in two hundred or three hundred in numbers riding briskly making fearsome noises cries and sounds thereby bringing in fear terrorizing the inmates of the Temples and the guards. These guards and temple priests numbering thousands were all heavyweights but did not have the grit so as to face the invaders what may come. The propaganda and fearsome cries of the invading armies made these temple people run off to forests enabling the invaders to plunder the temples of all riches and after desanctifying the temple they went away. If the temple priests and others outnumbering the invaders maybe tenfold had the grit to take up a stick and stand sternly to face the invaders numbering say two or three hundred they could have easily defeated the evil invaders and saved the temple and its riches for posterity. But comrades these people did not see to the wellbeing and strength of their bodies. They were concerned only with their supposed pseudo-spiritual welfare hence they could not ward off the attack on their culture of Dharm life's ways by the evil forces of The Mohamedans. This is what will happen if one does not give adequate attention and care to sustain one's body and mind in a proper righteous way. So comrades pay attention to your body well as your soul ensuring that you progress to yonder levels in peace and happiness in body and soul intact. These are perceptions cropping up on a perusal by a curious mind intending to decipher the ways and means to safeguard and adhere to Dharma in one's life's ways as Karma or day to day activities and deeds in life.There is no one who has not erred,sinned or comitted mistakes never mind the sins turn on a new chapter in life and decide to do only Good sticking to the righteous way of life and see the blissful happiness that it brings in including the igniting of the radiant powers of Godliness within oneself .

In conclusion of these perceptions intended for the betterment of " Dharma in life's ways as Karma ", It will be not complete if one does not venture into the quintessence of the outcome that enures on one's adhering to Dharma in life as is manifesting from The Indian Epic Ramayana. Everyone Knows of Sree Ram. Ram's birthplace temple was also vandalized and plundered by The Mughal invaders from the Afghanistan side. The temple was as is a reality of History destroyed and a Mosque was built in Theron. It was only recently that The Supreme court of India held at The Ramjanbhoomi has to be given to Hindu organizations for building a Befitting Temple. The fight for regaining the Lost temple was fought valiantly in The Courts as well as the Supreme court of India as Dharma Yudha and won with accolades. This sands a landmark decision in consonance with the proclaimed motto or slogan of Supreme cour of India namely "Yadho Dharma Statho Jaya". Especially when one comes to know that The Holy Quran says that " God will not heed the prayer prayed from a disputed site". This being the Dharmic verses of the Holy Quran how can a person who professes to be a Muslim go about snatching others' temples and build mosques, Theron. How can be Mosques built on others' land snatched as the disputes will never end even if they say that this is their land. Muslims cannot if actually following Quran built Mosques on disputed sites as God will not heed a prayer prayed from a disputed site. If God will not heed the prayer from a particular site No temple can be built on that site. Anyone who has read Ramanaya knows that Sree Rama a pious Avathar who manifested on Earth so as to save Humanity from certain perils by showing a way in Dharmic ways of life has to endure innumerable difficulties in Dharmic ways of life. All difficulties were overcome in accordance with the principles of Dharma. Sree ram's wife Sita was stolen by Ravan and taken to Lanka. She was put up at Asokavanam. It's said that Ravana had a curse that if he touches a lady without her consent his head will burst and he will die. Sre Rama and the army of Vanaras pursued Ravan for regaining Sita Devi. They reached Danushkodi and were confronted with the sea of Indian ocean that separated them from Lanka where Sita Devi was held captive. Sree Ram and The vanara Army (Army of Monkeys) started building a bridge to lanks so that they could march to Lanka and regain Sree Ramns Wife Sita Devi. While all were engrossed in building the bridge vigorously. Sree Rama and Lakshmana while sitting at a place and watching the progress of the bridge-building, saw a squirrel jump into the ocean in the place where the bridge is being built. The squirrel after jumping into the ocean swan back and then rolled itself in the soil and on the soil getting struck on its body it went and jumped again in the ocean and swan back. This the squirrel was repeating on and on so as to enable what little the squirrel could do in depositing solid to build the bridge for a righteous purpose of Sre Ram. Sre ram was soo taken over by these pious dees of even the measly squirrel in helping build the bridge to Lanka for a Righteous cause Sree Ram lovingly moved his fingers from head to tail end of the squirrel and lo there came the beautiful lines on the back of The squirrel. Thus comrade the quintessential effect of Strictly adhering to Dharma in life's ways as karma is that even the other entities and beings of the world will do whatever they can in one's quest and purposes of Dharma. This is Dharma in life's ways as Karmas. God is with Good,

Dharma, or Righteousness. With Righteousness or Dharma adhered to strictly God's Splendor and radiant power will permeate pervade and spill out in Aurora and splendor taking one to lofty heights of progress as is contemplated. Just take a vow to go by Dharma and adhere to it strictly with some times of strict adherence a tingling sensation will start to ignite from the bottom tip of one's spine slowly rising up and outshooting out of one's head falling like a fountain onto one's head. This is the beginning of the igniting of the power of Godliness. Evil deeds bring in Satan whose abode is Hell. As God will take disciples endearing to Heaven. Satan will surely take one who is dear to Him to Hell where it's surely pathetic, decadence in miseries, agony, and pain.

Gadhadharan Punathil
Punathil house, Manipuram lane
Nadakav, Calicut-673011
Kerala State,India

9 798886 672947

Printed by Libri Plureos GmbH in Hamburg,
Germany